Dreamers and DOERS

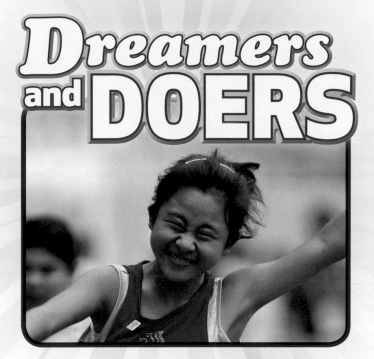

By M. C. Hall

Scott Foresman
is an imprint of

Glenview, Illinois • Boston, Massachusetts • Chandler, Arizona •
Upper Saddle River, New Jersey

Photographs

Every effort has been made to secure permission and provide appropriate credit for photographic material. The publisher deeply regrets any omission and pledges to correct errors called to its attention in subsequent editions.

Unless otherwise acknowledged, all photographs are the property of Pearson Education, Inc.

Photo locators denoted as follows: Top (T), Center (C), Bottom (B), Left (L), Right (R), Background (Bkgd)

Opener: GRIN/NASA
1 ©Diego Azubel/Corbis
3 ©Hulton Archive/Getty Images
4 ©Hulton Archive/Getty Images
5 Corbis
6 ©Hulton Archive/Getty Images
7 ©Bettmann/Corbis
8 ©Bettmann/Corbis
9 ©IOC/Allsport/Getty Images
10 GRIN/NASA
11 NASA
12 ©Diego Azubel/Corbis

ISBN 13: 978-0-328-46925-3
ISBN 10:   0-328-46925-4

3 4 5 6 7 8 9 10 V010 13 12 11 10

Do you dream of being a star athlete? That was Jim Thorpe's goal. He was good at football, baseball, and track.

Thorpe became a professional athlete. He made money by playing baseball. Then in 1912, Thorpe won two Olympic gold medals. At that time, professional athletes could not be in the Olympics. The Olympics Commission took back his medals.

Thorpe felt bad about losing the medals, but he didn't give up. He went on to play baseball for the New York Giants. He also played football and acted in movies. In 1982, the Olympics Commission gave the medals back to Thorpe's family.

Jackie Robinson was also good at many sports. His goal was to be a professional baseball player. However, at that time he could only play on an African American team.

In 1947, Jackie was hired by the Brooklyn Dodgers. He became the first African American player in Major League Baseball. Jackie helped the Dodgers win many games.

Wilma Rudolph wore a brace on one leg. Her goal was to walk without the brace. She reached that goal when she was nine years old.

Wilma became a star in basketball and track. In 1960, she won three Olympic gold medals! Wilma was the first American woman to win three medals at one Olympics!

Sally Ride was a good tennis player. She dreamed about becoming a sports star. Then Ride changed her goal.

She joined the U.S. space program. In 1983, Ride became the first woman to go into space.

Big dreams take a lot of hard work to come true. You can begin by setting goals and planning how to reach them. What you can dream about, you can do!